THE NOT SO STARVING ARTIST

For My Dad

THE NOT SO STARVING ARTIST

"I love money. I love everything about it. I bought some pretty good stuff. Got me a $300 pair of socks. Got a fur sink. An electric dog polisher. A gasoline powered turtleneck sweater. And, of course, I bought some dumb stuff, too." –Steve Martin

"An investment in knowledge pays the best interest." –Benjamin Franklin

TABLE OF CONTENTS

Chapters

Chapter One

Introduction

This book has been a long time coming. I'm pretty sure I've tried to write it at least a dozen times, but every time I started I'd get to a certain point and convince myself that I wasn't qualified enough, or that the world didn't need a book about finances for artists, musicians, actors, dancers and any other profession where job security is more scarce than a rent controlled NYC apartment. Now, regardless of whether or not the World may not need another financial book, the truth is that those of us with careers in the Arts do need a comprehensive guide to our finances. I'm tired of seeing my friends and colleagues struggle under the weight of credit card debt and student loans, and then, if they do manage to become debt free, wonder what to do with their money. I'm tired of seeing my friends live paycheck to paycheck and barely make ends meet. And I'm definitely tired of seeing my friends bust their butts at day jobs to pay the bills while they pursue their dreams. There has to be a better way. There has to be an easier way. Let me tell you there is, and that's what we are going to explore in this book. I've had enough conversations with my friends and co-workers to know that Artists don't usually know what to do when it comes to their finances. I also don't necessarily think that that's all on us. Artists seem to have been largely ignored by the financial industry. Maybe it's because society is trained to think that we don't make any money or maybe it's because our employment status can fluctuate from one month to the next, but regardless of the reason, we seem to have been left alone to figure out how to navigate our finances. I also think things like credit scores, real estate, the stock market, mortgages, and money market accounts can be intimidating for Artists to approach and learn about. I wouldn't go near the stock market for a long time simply because I didn't feel like I knew enough about it to make a smart decision with my money. I don't want a lack of financial knowledge to keep you from doing great things with the money you make in the Arts. I want to empower you to get out of debt and start planning for your future. I want to help you understand the different ways to invest your money, and feel like you are in control of your financial destiny.

"But he doesn't know the territory!", you and Charlie Cowell (the anvil salesman from Meredith Wilson's "The Music Man") might say. While I'm not selling boys bands, I am giving you financial advice and as Mayor Shinn liked to remind Harold Hill, it's important for you to see some credentials (Ok I got The Music Man references out of my system). For your consideration I present my qualifications (or lack thereof): I'm just an ordinary guy who makes his living as an actor (Jersey Boys, Motown the Musical, Spamalot). I don't have a degree in finance and I never went to business school. I was however, trained from a very young age to know what to do with my money. As a 28yr old I own and manage four rental properties worth over 1.2 million dollars (All bought with money I made as an Artist), I invest in the stock market and have consistently made money even when the market was down. I have zero credit card and student loan debt and impeccable credit. My real estate investments generate enough money so that I don't have to have a day job while I live in NYC. Let me say that again. I don't have to work a day job in NYC which means that I can focus all my time on my career in the Arts. I also know that if I can do any of this so can you! Money is a tool, and I want to help you put yours to work for you so that you too can focus all your time and energy on your Art.

I didn't, however, always have my current views about money. For a long time, my best idea was to save everything I made after expenses when I was working and then live off that money for as long as I could once I became unemployed. While this way of thinking was better than living "hand to mouth" and spending every dollar I made, it still meant that at some point the money would run out and I'd be back to square one. By just saving I still wasn't going to reach full financial independence, and while keeping me free to focus on my career in the Arts, I was just delaying being broke or being forced to get some sort of non-performing job. It wasn't until I booked Jersey Boys that I realized that there could be a better way of doing things. I looked at someone like my dad, a semi-retired Real Estate broker, but still able to do what he wanted without worrying about how he was going to pay for it. By doing some digging he let me in on how he did it: Investing. I knew he and my mom had owned several rental properties back in the day, but now he was living off the investments he had made in the stock market. Those investments were bringing in enough to live off of and then some. Seeing this sparked the desire for me to become independent of a fickle business like Show Business. No matter what my work situation was, I would be able to live off solid investments and have all the time in the world to focus on a career in the Arts. I often joke now about being "retired", but all that really means is that I can live in one of the most expensive cities on the planet free from depending on contracts as an actor. I'm also building an infrastructure that can support me now and continue to support me when I do decide to stop working someday. I also realize this is a journey. Look, even if your investments subsidize (pay part of) your rent and living expenses a little in the beginning you are still way ahead of the curve! Taking baby steps and knocking down your day to day expenses with money you make from investments is better than doing nothing at all. Hey, when I bought my first rental property, I was bringing in about $800/month in profit after expenses. While not enough to live off of, it sure did feel good to know that I had extra money coming in to help pay for my life in NYC. It also felt good to be able to say "no" to things. So often

THE NOT SO STARVING ARTIST

as Artists we have to take jobs we don't necessarily want to do, but we need the money so saying "yes" seems to be our only option. You still might have to agree, in the beginning, to take jobs you would rather turn down, but I guarantee that as you continue to invest and bring in revenue from other sources, you will get to the point where "no" is a viable option. So without further ado, here is everything I know about finance, money management, and investing and everything I think you should too.

Chapter Two

Debt: Credit Cards, Interest, and Student Loans - Oh my!

I figured we should jump right in to the thing that I see my friends and coworkers dealing with the most: Debt. Debt can do some nasty things to your finances and leave you feeling like you will never get out of the hole you're in. Debt can hurt your credit score and keep you from being able to qualify for a home loan or rent a really great apartment. Being in debt sucks, but I'm here to tell you that by being consistent with a few good financial habits, you can get yourself out of debt and never ever have to go back!

First up: **Credit Cards**.

Credit card debt is the most common kind of debt plaguing consumers in this country. Why? It's almost unavoidable. Our economy runs on credit cards, and as technology continues to change the way we shop, it seems more and more electronic money will make paper currency extinct. How much debt does the average U.S. household have? A whopping $7,000. And then, if we look at only the household claiming to be in debt that number jumps to $15,000. Yikes. As Artists, credit cards can be dangerous because of our lack of job security. Buying something today, only to have a show close or contract end tomorrow, spells trouble (With a capital "T" and that rhymes with "P"...ok I swear I'm done now) and an outstanding balance on a credit card you might not be able to pay off. The first thing you need to do to get yourself out of credit card debt is to really examine your spending. If you know how/why you ended up in debt in the first place, you will be able to figure out the necessary steps to get yourself out. As a child I was taught that you don't buy things you can't afford i.e. pay for with cash on the spot, and that lesson must have stuck because I actually didn't own a credit card before 2011. I used my debit card or paid with cash. Why? I never wanted to be in a position where I was tempted to buy something I couldn't afford. I also hated being forced to be a part of a broken system. Credit card companies do their best to get you in debt and keep you in debt, but you can't have a credit history or high credit score without them. Oy. While not owning a credit card was fairly drastic, it kept me honest about my purchasing habits and out of debt. While I'm no longer anti credit card, (they can actually be an excellent tool: they can help you earn a good credit score and some of them have pretty great rewards programs) I am still wary of the consequences of their misuse. You might not even be aware of the little things you are doing to keep yourself in debt, but taking a closer look at your credit card bill will help shed some light on your spending habits. My credit card even has a nifty way to see my spending by category so I can see where my money is going. Once you know where your money is going, you should be able to set limits for yourself for each individual category. You must also determine the difference between needs and wants.

THE NOT SO STARVING ARTIST

I think it's safe to say that we are a part of a "wants" based spending culture in the U.S. I mean, hell, getting consumers to spend money on "wants", or need based wants is a huge part of what capitalism is all about. From the moment we can watch TV, we are bombarded with ads telling us what we need to buy and where to spend our hard earned money. I find a lot of my friends in the Arts try to keep up with the most current fashion and technology trends, but wind up with a lot of credit card debt or a zero balance in their savings account. I'm not advocating living like you are in the 1900's but I do think there needs to be a balance. For example, you may need a car, but the type and newness of that car heads into "wants" territory. True needs are things like food, shelter, clothing, and health insurance. Wants are things like new clothes, entertainment, and vacations. Again, I don't think it's wrong to want nice things, you just need to be able to afford them! I want you to get to the point where you are bringing in so much money that you can afford the nice things you want, but in the beginning your needs should get first priority when it comes to your spending. On a deeper level, your needs have to be able to be met by what you bring home. For example, if you make $2000 a month and your rent is $1900, you've probably let some need based wants take you into the danger zone. The solution? You need to find a cheaper apartment, get a roommate, or get a second job. Yes, you need a place to sleep, but $100 to eat for a month isn't going to work. It's all about give and take. If you have to live on the Upper West Side in NYC, maybe find a two or three bedroom and split the cost with friends. Or if living alone is more important to you, find a nice studio in Inwood or Washington Heights. What I'm saying is, KEEP YOUR OVERHEAD LOW. No, I'm not talking about apartments with short ceilings. Your "overhead" is the amount of money it costs you to live. Food, rent, transportation, health insurance, etc. The lower you keep the costs the easier it will be to stay out of debt. I also advise putting at least 10% of whatever you make after taxes into savings. The bigger the safety net you can create in your savings account the better you will feel (and better off you'll be!) anytime you find yourself unemployed.

Interest: keeping you in debt

The benefit to sending in extra payments on any debt, is that those extra payments will help shrink the amount of interest you will pay on that debt. I'll explain: These days, most credit cards compound their interest on a daily basis, not monthly. For example, let's say you have a revolving balance of $10,000 on your credit card, and your daily interest rate is 0.041 (which is about the same as an APR or Annual (interest) Percentage Rate of 15%). Multiply $10,000 by 0.00041 and you get $4.10 which means that you'd pay $4.10 on the first day. On the second day, your balance would be $10,004.10, and you'd pay interest on that total. Pretty scary stuff, but you can avoid paying more in interest by getting that balance down. while you are paying off your credit card I would also suggest going to an all cash system to make sure you don't add to your cc balance. Once you are out of debt, do everything in your power to stay out of debt. I pay off my credit in full every month. I also get 2% cash back for doing so, and if you have a good credit score you can qualify for some great rewards cards with no annual fee. Make sure you always read the fine print so you don't end up paying an annual fee for your credit card. What about the interest rate? I never bother worrying about the APR because I'm always going to pay off my balance every month. I also make sure I have the "auto pay" setting switched on. That way, even if I forget to pay the bill the minimum payment will get sent and I'll avoid paying interest.

Student Loans

There's a tongue in cheek line in the Musical Pippin where King Charlemagne turns to the audience and says, "Sometimes I wonder if the fornicating I'm getting is worth the fornicating I'm getting." I want you to take the same look at the financial cost of attending a college for musical theater or any arts based degree. I.e. is what you are paying for, worth what you are spending? Full disclosure: I refused to take out student loans to get my BFA in Musical Theater from the Boston Conservatory. Why? At the time I wasn't willing to go into debt for a degree in Musical Theater. While I appreciate and understand the value of having a college degree, (heck, you can't even donate sperm without being a college graduate) I have a hard time seeing the value of going deep into debt for a degree in a field that requires none. Obviously, anyone training for a career in the Arts is paying for more than just the diploma, but I would still pose this question: Is what you're paying for - training, diploma, connections, worth what you are paying? Could you spend less training elsewhere? When I did the math on what I was actually paying per hour per class at the Boston Conservatory, it came out to something crazy like $300/per 2hr class. I realized that I could spend far less by moving to NYC and training there. I don't in any way mean to bash getting your BFA, but I've never been asked for my diploma in an audition. I look at it this way: If you were going to be a plastic surgeon, the student loans make sense at least from the standpoint that you will most likely be able to pay them off once you start practicing medicine. But as Artists, we can be unemployed for months, sometimes years at a time, not knowing how we will pay our rent, let alone trying to deal with massive student loans. For those of you who already have student loans, let me encourage you to pay them off as fast as you can. Put aside 10% of your take home pay to send in extra payments and avoid paying extra interest. If you happen to get a high paying job, take out a big chunk of those loans before splurging on something you want. The rule to live by still applies: Get out of debt as fast as you can and never ever go back.

Another word on Student Loans and BFA's: We are working with a broken system. The cost of college in this country has gotten so expensive that it's hard to logically justify the cost of most degrees. That said, getting your degree is important, especially if you want to teach later down the road. The reason for sharing my views on not going into debt for my BFA in Musical Theater is to help you to see the big picture. I actually investigated finishing my degree while I was on tour with Jersey Boys because I do see the value in having that diploma. I just wasn't willing to compromise my financial future for it. I think so often we go along with things because "that's just how it's done", but, especially in the Arts, there isn't one "right" path to having a career. I've worked with performers over the years who graduated high school and moved right to NYC, as well as those who went to college for their chosen Artistic profession. Just know why you are doing what you are doing and how much it's going to cost you so that there aren't any surprises down the line.

Chapter Three

Credit Scores

It seems every time I turn on the TV there is bound to be a commercial about whether or not I know what my credit score is. While the commercials can be annoying, their message is an important one. In fact, knowing your credit score is very very important! But knowing what your credit looks like is just the first step. You must also understand the factors that affect your credit and understand how to fix it if it's lower than it should be. Making sure you have good credit will insure you are able to buy a house, or get a job (some employers even do credit checks before hiring nowadays). If you've seen the same commercials I have, you know that there are a plethora of companies that will help you see your credit score. True to their word, Credit Karma will let you see your Credit profile for free, so log on and check out what you're working with. If your credit falls in the Good (680 - 719) or Excellent

(720 and above) range, Congratulations and keep up the good work. If you have Average (620 - 679), Poor (580 - 619), or Very Poor (579 and below) credit let's figure out how to get that score back up to where it should be.

Things that affect your credit score

Your credit score is determined by a few factors and it's important to know what those are. In addition, each factor affects your score differently (some factors are more important than others) From creditkarma.com:

Open Credit Card Utilization Rate

Your open credit card utilization rate is your available credit compared with how much you're using at any given time. It can be calculated by taking your total open credit card balances and dividing that number by your total open credit card limits. The resulting percentage is your utilization rate.

It's important to note that your credit card utilization rate is not calculated by looking at the balance you carry over from month to month. It is calculated using the balance you have at the time that your credit card issuer reports to the credit bureau. Therefore, it is not necessary to carry over a balance from month to month. You could maintain a healthy credit card utilization through regular credit card use and paying off your balance every month.

Percent of On Time Payments

Your percentage of on-time payments represents how often you make payments on time. It's often a **heavily weighted** factor in calculating a credit score, so just one or two late payments could significantly affect your score.

Paying bills on time is one of the best ways to keep up good credit health; it shows lenders and creditors that you're reliable and will pay back your debts.

Number of Derogatory Marks

These include accounts in collections, bankruptcies, foreclosures and liens. Your credit score will be **severely negatively affected** by a derogatory mark on your credit report. Derogatory marks typically take seven to ten years to clear from credit history, and they generally cannot be removed earlier.

A derogatory mark could severely influence your chances of getting approved for credit; it indicates to a lender that you may have significantly mismanaged credit in the past.

Average Age of Open Credit Lines

This factor averages the ages of your open credit cards, mortgages, auto loans, student loans and other lines of credit on your credit report. If your credit history is lengthy, lenders have more information to accurately assess creditworthiness.

It's also frequently an indication that you have been able to successfully manage your credit.

For this reason, closing your oldest credit card account is typically ill-advised. It will shorten the average length of your open credit lines and reduce your available credit, possibly increasing your credit utilization rate. Think carefully about when you may want to close an old credit card account, and when you may want to avoid doing so.

Total Number of Accounts

This credit score factor totals up your number of credit cards, auto and student loans, mortgages and other lines of credit. Consumers with a higher number of credit accounts generally have better credit scores, since they've been approved for credit by more lenders. Also, having various types of credit--both revolving and installment--on your profile can positively contribute to your creditworthiness.

However, it's typically not recommended to open several new lines of credit simply to increase your total number of credit accounts. This factor of your credit score is usually weighed **less heavily** than the rest. If you are in the market to apply for new credit, make sure you first read reviews and research which product is right for you.

Total Hard Credit Inquiries

The final factor commonly used in your credit score is your total number of hard credit inquiries. Hard inquiries occur when a financial institution, such as a lender or credit card issuer, checks your credit in order to decide whether to approve you for a loan or credit card. A hard inquiry may occur when you apply for any of the following:

Auto loan
Student loan
Business loan
Personal loan
Credit card

Mortgage

One hard inquiry could negatively affect your credit score by a few points, but the effect typically will begin to lessen after a couple of months. Multiple hard inquiries generally will more significantly impact your credit score, and can communicate to lenders that you are desperate for credit or are unable to qualify for credit. For this reason, **it's a good idea to avoid applying for several lines of credit at once**.

Chapter Four

Budgeting 101

One of the biggest issues I see my friends dealing with when it comes to their spending is that they don't really know how much they spend. If you are unaware of what you really spend on a monthly basis you will never be able to get yourself out of debt. The good news is that with some simple math you can figure out where all your money is going. I'm going to give you a few steps on how know your numbers and use that knowledge to make a plan to get your spending under control:

1. **Put the credit card down.** Credits cards make it way too easy to lose track of what you spend so for a full month you need to go to an all cash system. You won't have to do this forever, but until you have a handle on what you're spending, limiting yourself to a strict all cash budget will help you become an expert

budgeter. I'll explain more about how this will work

2. **Sit down and write out what you spend**. First start with fixed costs like rent, cell phone (base amount, not what you may end up paying in overages) health care premiums, insurance, transportation, etc. Next, do averages for things like utilities, cell phone overages, transportation overages, entertainment, any sort of business expenses (voice lessons, dance class, acting class, art supplies, etc). How do you get the average? Say you want to find the average amount you spend on utilities: Take your utility bills for the last six months and add all the numbers together. Next, divide that grand total by six and you should get your average monthly utility cost. Unsure about what you've spent? Most, if not all, banks and credit cards make it very easy to look up your account activity. I do almost all my banking online and can easily see what's coming in and going out at all times with a few clicks on my laptop.

3. **Write down what you make**. Total up all the money you bring in monthly, and this should be after taxes, because you can't count on money that's already been taken out of your paycheck.
4. **Compare the lists**. If what you spend is greater than what you make, not only are you not going to be able to get out of debt, but you are actually getting deeper into it.
5. **Reevaluate**. I'm going to give you percentages of what you should be spending on different categories to help you figure out where you've gone astray.

Housing: 35%
Utilities: 5%
Food: 10-20%
Transportation: 15-20%
Clothing: 3-5%
Medical: 3%
Entertainment: 5-10%
Savings: 5-10%
Debt repayment: 5-15%

THE NOT SO STARVING ARTIST

To further illustrate what this looks like, here are some real number examples to help you see how to break your expenses down by category. Also, you can use the following equations to figure out these percentages: Your Salary / 100 = 1% of your salary. In the example we are going to use, your salary is represented by $3700 a month (The average NYC waiter makes roughly $933/wk). So the formula looks like this: $3700 / 100 = $37. $37 is one percent of your monthly salary. All we do now is multiply our $37 or 1% by whatever percentage necessary per category.

Housing. So if your take home pay for the month is $3700 and you are trying to stay within spending 35% of your salary on housing, that means that you should be spending about $1295/month in rent. Impossible in NYC? not necessarily, but depending on where you live you may need to adjust your percentage. NOTE: spending more on rent means you have to cut back somewhere else. You can't up your housing percentage without taking it away from another category. Like I said before, if your rent is eating up too much of your salary, you may need to explore having a roommate or two or finding a cheaper apartment.

Utilities. 5% of $3700 is $185. This number should include cable, wifi, and your cell phone.

Food. At 3.7k in take home pay, you should be spending anywhere from $370 - $740/month on food. Groceries are really the best way to keep your food costs under control. I know Seamless is great, but $15 a meal is going to leave you way over budget.

Transportation. $555 is 15% of $3700. A monthly unlimited Metrocard is $116 so you could potentially spend way less than 15%. If you have a car, that $555 is probably more accurate.

Clothing. $111 - $185 a month puts you in the 3-5% range, BUT I don't know a lot of people who need new clothes every month. Putting this money into savings or towards your debt is a much better use than putting the latest fashions into your closet.

Medical. $111 can go towards your medical costs every month. As a union actor, I have Cigna Heath Insurance provided by Actors Equity. My monthly health care cost comes out to about $34 a month (my yearly premium is $400). Thankfully, as Artists, we have access to cheaper health care via the affordable care act, so if you find yourself unemployed, take advantage of government subsidized health care. Once you've paid your health care premiums, do your best to stay healthy and put whatever money you have left over into savings if you can. You can always draw on it if you have to go to the doctor or have unexpected medical costs.

Entertainment. $185 - $370. The really great part about spending money on Entertainment as Artists, is that you can write most of it off on your taxes. For example, as an actor, any movie or play I see can be written off as "research". I would imagine the same would apply to tickets to an art museum or concert for visual artists and musicians respectively. Again, whatever you can save from this category can go towards debt repayment and/or savings.

Savings. $185 - $370. For me saving 10% is the minimum. I'll touch on this more in the chapter on Saving.

Debt Repayment. $185 - $555. If you are in debt, I highly recommend putting as much of your salary as possible towards paying it off. As I said earlier, the quicker you pay down the balance on your loans and credit card debt, the less you'll pay in the long run in interest. And just think, once you are debt free that 5-15% can be put towards savings or some of the fun investment options we are going to explore in this book.

I hope this gives you a clear idea of what it looks like to break down your expenses by percentages and helps you to see how to know what you should be spending on each different category.

6. **Back to that part about an all cash system**. Once you've figured out what you should be spending on each category per month, put each amount into separate envelopes and only pull from the appropriate envelope to pay for things in that category. Yes, this requires planning on your part, but it will really help you stick to a budget and show you how to retrain some of your bad spending habits.

7. **Evaluate your performance**. How did you do with the all cash system for a month? Did you run out of money in any of the envelopes before the month was up? Was it because the percentage was too low or because you are overspending in that category?

I'll even go one step further and make you a blank chart that you can use to keep track of your month to month finances, Here you go:

THE NOT SO STARVING ARTIST

MY MONEY MAP

WHAT I BRING HOME AFTER TAXES PER WEEK

WEEK 1:_____

WEEK 2:_____

WEEK 3:_____

WEEK 4:_____

TOTAL EARNINGS: _____

10% FOR SAVINGS:_____

MY FIXED COSTS

RENT:_____

AVERAGE UTILITIES:_____

THE NOT SO STARVING ARTIST

TRANSPORTATION:_____

AVERAGE PHONE/INTERNET:_____

INSURANCE (medical/hazard):_____
DEBT REPAYMENT:_____

VARIABLE COSTS

GROCERIES:_____
EATING OUT:_____

ENTERTAINMENT:_____

MISCELLANEOUS (clothes, business expenses, etc):_____

TOTALS

TOTAL INCOME AFTER TAXES/
SAVINGS:_____

—

TOTAL FIXED COSTS:_____

TOTAL VARIABLE COSTS:_____

=

AMOUNT LEFT OVER:_____

How do you get to Carnegie Hall? Practice. The same thing applies to getting a good grip on your finances. Follow the steps I outlined above and fill in the chart with your specific numbers until you don't need to. I.e. after a few months you will know exactly where your money is going and won't have to write everything down anymore. I promise if you do the work and can stick to living within your means, you will be on your way to taking control of your financial future.

Also, what I've outlined above is a rough idea of what your money map should look like. Obviously feel free to customize it to whatever your individual expenses look like. There are several of the same charts in the back of the book so that you can continue to chart your expenses for as long as you need to.

Chapter Five

Save, Save, Save

Do you remember those analogies they had on the SAT's? How about this one: Debt : The Dark Side :: Saving : _____? The Shapoopi. The answer we were looking for was The Shapoopi. (Ok this is the last Music Man reference for real, I swear) All joking aside, Saving your money is an important part of being financially stable. And beyond financial stability, saving will help you build up a safety net for when you find yourself unemployed. As Artists we really can't rely on any sort of Arts job for stability. Obviously there are exceptions, long running Broadway Shows, The Met, ABT for dancers, and becoming the next Pablo Picasso. But if you are like most of us, working in the Arts can mean long periods of unemployment and vastly different salaries from job to job. Saving your money consistently no matter what sort of pay you are making is a great habit that will set you up for financial success. In the chapter on debt, I mentioned putting at least 10% of your take home pay into savings and I'll reiterate that here. The goal should be to have about six months living expenses in savings as your safety net. I would go even further to say that because of our fluctuating employment statuses as Artists, eight or nine months living expenses in savings would be even better. It may seem daunting to live on 90% of what you bring home, but having a nice safety net will save you an immeasurable amount of worry in the long run. I also want to stress that 10% is just a jumping off point. If you can keep your living expenses low and save more, do it! It's really all about being able to find the balance of a sustainable lifestyle. I can't tell you how many of my friends book high paying contracts, adjust their lifestyles to match their new income and then find themselves in financial trouble when those jobs end. Had they found a happy medium and continued to live at a sustainable level while earning more, they would've ended up in a much better place financially when they found themselves unemployed. I also understand that what I'm saying may be a radical change from what you know or how you live now, but retraining yourself to become a saver will pay off, pun intended, in the long run.

Which savings account is best?

The kind of savings account you decide to put your money is also important. I use Capital One 360 as my savings account. Why? Interest rates. All banks will offer you a perk in the form of interest for "investing" your money with them, but those rates can be vastly different depending on the bank. Most normal savings accounts at banks like Wells Fargo, Bank of America, Chase, etc., will give you a 0.01% annual return on the money you keep in savings. For example: If you had $1000 in savings, at 0.01%, you would earn 1 penny in interest for the year. Oh boy. Compare that to the current rate at Capital One 360, 0.75% annually and, while it's not amazing, $7.50/year on your $1000 sure as heck beats one penny! Interest rates can fluctuate from time to time (when I opened the account back in 2008 the rate was at 5%!!) The only drawback to Capital One 360 is that it's an online only bank, but the interest rate is so great that I don't mind transferring money in and out of my other bank accounts. Another great savings account is a Money Market Account. Unlike Capital One 360, which requires no minimum balance, most Money Market accounts will require a certain amount to be kept in your account at all times. From what I've seen in the last few years, few Money Market accounts can match the rate at Capital One 360 and it doesn't really make sense to deal with that minimum balance nonsense.

Saving for Retirement

Saving for your retirement is an extremely important part of money management and the best way to make sure you have money put away for the day you no longer want to work. Keep in mind that the money you put into any sort of 401k or retirement account will most likely have to stay there until you turn 65, though there are exceptions to that rule with accounts like a Roth IRA (which I'll explain in more detail). Also be aware that for most retirement accounts you won't pay taxes until you actually start withdrawing money at retirement age! Typical types of retirement accounts include:

401k: A 401k is a retirement savings plan sponsored by an employer. It lets workers save and invest a piece of their paycheck before taxes are taken out. Taxes aren't paid until the money is withdrawn from the account. credit: Wall Street Journal

Roth IRA: A Roth IRA is an individual account allowing a person to set aside after-tax income up to a specified amount each year. Provided the account has been open for five years, both earnings on the account and withdrawals after age 59 1/2 are tax-free. Also, under age 59 1/2 you are allowed to withdraw the exact amount of money you have contributed, penalty free. However, the account must be open for five years to do so.

I currently have both kinds of accounts and as a member of Actors Equity Association my employers pay a sum equal to 3% of my weekly salary into my 401k. Investing into my Roth IRA is on me and I believe the current annual cap on deposits is around $5500. In addition to both these retirement accounts, members of IASTE, AEA, SAG, AFTRA, AGVA, and AFM can also qualify for pensions through their unions.

Basically, I used to think that saving my money while working and then living off those savings when a show closed was the best way to go. While making sure you have a good safety net is always important, living off your savings until they run out will always put you back to where you started. What about moving forward? Buying a house? Having kids? Retirement? It wasn't until I realized that I needed to start to set myself up for the future that any of those things became viable realities. Even if you don't want to buy a house or have kids, wouldn't it be nice to be able to support yourself without relying on a day job or depending on the Arts. This is where investing comes in. Investing your money is the key to putting it to "work" for you, instead of just letting it sit in a bank account.

Chapter Six

Investing 101

Ok so now that we've talked about saving, let's move on to other ways to grow the money you are making. Investing your money is the best thing you can do to help it grow and start to make money for you. Again, I have to give credit to my dad for helping me understand the importance of investing. When I was a kid, my dad thought it would be fun to teach my brothers and me about the stock market. He gave us each $500 (pretend money) and told us to pick stocks to invest in. He then tracked our progress for six months and gave us the results of who "won" (made the most money on their initial investment). My brothers and I of course picked companies like McDonalds, Disney, and even IBM. Now I have no idea who "won" or even which stocks I picked as a ten year old, but the experiment stuck with me as something that was important. Full Disclosure: I don't love the stock market. Again I feel like it's another broken system and I'll give you an example why: A few years ago Lionsgate studios was releasing one of the Hunger Games sequels. The smartsy fartsy market analysts predicted it would gross 97 million in its opening weekend. When the movie came out, however, it only grossed 94 million. Lionsgate stock went down. Um, what?? For me this is crazy town. A company can have an exceptional opening weekend at the box office, but because some guy on Wall Street thinks it should've done better the company (and it's stock holders) lose money? No thank you. As I said in the opening, I do invest in the Stock Market, but in something called a mutual fund, and I'll explain more on that later. What I want you understand from the experiment my dad had us do is that the sooner you can start understanding how to invest, the better off you will be. A good rule of thumb is to not go beyond 10% of you net worth in any one investment. What's your net worth? Your net worth is calculated by adding up all the assets you have (house, bank accounts, stocks, etc) and then subtracting any liabilities (debt, loans). For example, say you own a home or apartment (assets) worth $300k and have $20k in the bank. Add those two together for a total of $320k in assets. The remaining balance of the mortgage on your home is $200k and you have a student loan balance of $20k (liabilities). Subtract your liabilities, or $220k, from the total of your assets, $320k, and you get a net worth of $100k, and if you are going to follow the 10% rule with this example, you wouldn't want to exceed more than $10k in any one investment.

Types of common investments.

1. **Stocks**. The stock market can be a great way to invest your money, but has been proven to be the most lucrative over the long term. Your money is fairly liquid (explained below) while in the stock market.
2. **Real Estate**. My personal favorite and another great way to invest your money. I like real estate because I feel like I'm always getting

something tangible as opposed to something like stocks that exist in cyberspace. Not super liquid.

3. **Small Businesses**. A great way to invest, but this one can get very tricky and requires some serious research and devotion. Not super liquid.

4. **Bonds**. A bond is a debt security, similar to an I.O.U. When you purchase a bond you are lending money to the "issuer". In return for that money the issuer provides you with a bond in which it promises to pay a specified interest rate during the lifetime of the bond and to repay the face value when it matures, or comes due. Basically you buy a bond and wait for it to mature. Each bond matures at a certain rate and after a specific amount of time. Can be liquid, but selling a bond before it matures defeats the purpose of buying it in the first place.

5. **CD's**. CD's are essentially glorified savings accounts with a few restrictions. They require a minimum investment and minimum amount

of time the money must be left in the account. you can get your money out before that minimum amount of time, but you will have to pay a penalty to do so. The interest rates I've seen in the last few years aren't worth tying up your money for a long time. Not liquid.

6. **Precious metals/diamonds**. This is exactly what it sounds like. Buy some gold, put it in a safe and wait until the market value goes up. You can also buy stock in commodities like precious metals and oil. Actual gold in your safe: Not liquid, Stocks in Commodities: same liquidity as stocks.

Before you dive right in, make sure you do some investigating on any type of investment that interests you. I read many an "Investing for Dummies" book before committing any of my cold hard cash to any sort of investment.

Factors to consider when making an investment.

Liquidity: Liquidity refers to how easily you can access and withdraw your money. Money in a bank account is the most liquid kind of investment, especially when it's linked to a debit card. But money, say, in Real Estate isn't very liquid because you would have to sell the house to get your initial investment back. Liquidity is important because you need to know how long it will take or if you even can get your money out (without penalty) from an investment if you need it. It's also important to know how long you will probably need to leave your money in certain types of investments to make any money. Which leads us to...

Return on Investment: The return on investment is the % at which your money is going to multiply in any investment. Remember when we talked about the interest rates banks offer for you to keep your money in their accounts? That % is your return on investment. I'll give you some examples:

THE NOT SO STARVING ARTIST

Wells Fargo offers 0.01% APR (annual percentage rate) on their basic savings account so the return on "investing" my money in their bank account is .01% a year.

The rate in Capital One 360's saving account is .75% APR.

The stock market mutual fund I invest in produces at about 5.5% APR.

I own a rental property in Downtown Denver that produces at 7.00% APR. This number doesn't include the equity (amount of $$ value of the home) I've gained since purchasing the property and I'll explain how to figure the return on real estate investments in the section under real estate, but as you can start to see, the goal of any investment should be to get the highest return while keeping the risk involved relatively low.

Risk: Every investment comes with a certain amount of risk. Bank accounts pose the least amount of risk because they are usually backed by the government via the FDIC (Federal Deposit Insurance Corporation) up to $250,000 per investor. I.e. the money in your bank account is insured by the FDIC up to $250k. The risk involved with the stock market is greater simply because you and I don't have control over what stock prices may or may not do. Real Estate can also have many risks: the property can be vacant, things in the home can break, the housing market can fluctuate, etc. The amount of risk you are comfortable with is up to you, but just make sure you have done your due diligence so you have an idea of what you are getting yourself (and your money) into.

Putting Your Eggs In One Basket

You know the old saying, but how does that apply to investing? It's very dangerous to put all your money into one kind of investment. Spreading your money out over several different kinds of investments is commonly called diversification. For example: A diversified investment portfolio might include investments in the stock market, a rental property or two, and some stocks and bonds. This way, if something happens in one of your investments, you will still be ok because of your investments in other areas.

Exploring Investment Types

In the next few chapters, I'll dive deeper into a few types of investments that I've used to make my money work for me. As I said in the introduction, my goal has been to invest the money I make as an artist and let those investments support me anytime I find myself unemployed. (I like to think of it as my personal built in unemployment insurance.)

Chapter Seven

Real Estate

Boy do I love Real Estate. This love may stem from the fact that my father has been a real estate broker for the last thirty years, or maybe because I'm addicted to HGTV, but whatever the reason, real estate has been and continues to be my favorite kind of investment. I bought my first investment property after being on tour with Jersey Boys. I purchased a one bedroom, one bath in the heart of Downtown Denver. Denver? but what about NYC? Well, I really wanted to buy in NYC, but after running the numbers it didn't quite make sense. And beyond that, because of the way NYC real estate works, it can actually make more sense to rent in NYC instead of buying. Let me explain: As a renter in NYC, you only have to pay your utilities and rent, but the second you buy that same apartment you are now on the hook for the monthly maintenance fee, insurance, and taxes (all of which are MUCH higher than the same expenses elsewhere in the country) and then, depending on how much money you have for a downpayment, you will have to pay a mortgage. More often than not, these costs will all add up to way more than you would pay to rent the same apartment. I'll give you some real numbers from one of the properties in NYC I was looking at a few years ago:

When I was looking to buy an apartment in NYC back in the fall of 2013, I found a 300 sqft Co-Op studio apartment in Long Island City listed for $100,000. When I did some digging I discovered that the maintenance on this studio was a little over $700/month. Add about $2,000/year in taxes and $40/month for insurance and you are looking at about $900/month BEFORE even talking about what your mortgage could be. If you put 20% down ($20,000) and took a 30 year fixed mortgage on the rest ($80,000) at 5% interest you would be looking at a mortgage payment of $430/month. Add that to the other costs and you are paying roughly $1300/month to own that studio. Not bad, but lets continue. To purchase and live in an apartment in a Co-op building you have to be approved by the buildings board. But what if you want to buy as an investment? Most building's Co-Op boards have strict rules about leasing or subletting any units to non-owners. Most of the one's I found were something like "only three out of the nine units in the building may be subleased out at a time" So I guess if three units in the building already have tenants you are out of luck! Or "units must be owner occupied three out of every five years". On the numbers alone, if you were allowed to rent it out, you would maybe cover your expenses or even come up a little short (the average rent for a studio is about $1200/month), and if you did pay off the mortgage, you would essentially still be paying about $900 in "rent" with your other costs. If you have your heart set on buying an apartment in NYC, make sure you aren't paying considerably more than what you would be paying to rent the same apartment.

THE NOT SO STARVING ARTIST

Now let's compare this studio to what I ended up buying in Denver. I paid $161,500 cash (no mortgage, and I'll explain why I did that a little later) for a 700 sqft one bedroom, one bathroom loft in a historic building in the the heart of Downtown Denver. The loft was currently being used as a rental and I was able to keep that tenant in place. My monthly maintenance fee on the apartment was $214, the taxes were $917/year ($76/month), and the insurance came out to about $20/month. So all in, my monthly expenses were about $300/month. I was getting $1,250/month in rent from my tenant. $900/month in profit meant that this investment was earning at about 6.7% annually ($900 x 12 months / one percent of $161k which is $1615). But wait, it gets better. After holding the loft for two years, I sold it to my tenant for $220k. The instant profit of $60,000 comes out to a 37% return on my initial investment of $161k. So now, after two years my return on investment ends up at 50.35% (2 years at 6.7% = 13.4% + 37% from the sale = 50.35%). And that's why I love real estate so much, not only can it produce income for you while you rent it out, but you can also make a huge profit if you sell it at the right time!

Now back to why I didn't take a mortgage on the one bedroom loft? The short answer: I was about to leave my job at Jersey Boys and I wanted to make sure I was maximizing the profit I was making every month and at the same time minimizing my expenses. As Artists we never know when we will be unemployed, so I didn't want to be shelling out extra money every month for a place in Denver I wasn't living in. Yes, I still had a low monthly cost (the $214 maintenance fee), but because I owned it outright my monthly profit was much higher and I could use that profit to subsidize my rent in NYC. My older brother and I go back and forth about paying cash for real estate all the time, but he has a much more stable job than I do so he doesn't have to worry about covering the mortgages on his rentals if they should go unrented. His way of thinking makes sense from a more traditional real estate investing standpoint: buy several properties and let your tenants pay the mortgages. Your monthly profit may not be that high, or even exist, in the beginning, but you are essentially letting someone else pay for you to own the property. If we apply this way of thinking to what I did with the one bedroom, I COULD have taken that $161k and put 20% down payments on two or three properties. The profit margins would have been much lower, but I would now be the proud owner of three rentals. Again the reason I didn't do that is because that strategy carries a lot more risk, especially for someone with no real job security.

But just because I didn't take a mortgage on my first income property doesn't mean they are bad or that you shouldn't know all about them. Mortgages are actually a good kind of debt as long as you don't overextend yourself. Let's explore a few types now:

The fixed rate mortgage

A fixed rate mortgage is a mortgage where the interest rate you pay on the loan is fixed or locked for a set amount of time. Common terms are 30 years or 15 years. The benefit to this type of mortgage is that you will always know what your payment will be and a 30 year term will keep the payments relatively low. However, paying a loan back over 30 years means you will be paying a lot in interest. If the mortgage is on your primary residence, you should think about sending in extra payments to pay down the principal (actual amount you borrowed) to avoid some of that interest. If the mortgage is on a rental property hopefully you are cash flow positive (making more than your monthly expenses), and you can let the tenants pay down the mortgage.

The adjustable rate mortgage

An adjustable rate mortgage is a mortgage where the interest rate will change or adjust to stay in line with the current Federal interest rate. Usually with adjustable rate mortgages, the rate will stay the same for a set number of years and then start to adjust. Common terms are 3 and 7 years. Once the rate becomes adjustable there are usually set minimums of how much the rate will increase per year and maximums of how high the rate can actually go over the lifetime of the loan. Adjustable rate mortgages can be beneficial to anyone who doesn't plan on holding a property for a long period of time and they can also save you money because the interest rates can be lower than on a fixed rate mortgage.

Other factors when considering a mortgage

Not only do you want to investigate the interest rate on any loan, but you must look at what getting the loan may or may not cost you. Many mortgages require origination fees and other costs that will add to the amount of money you have to bring to the table to close on a house. In NYC real estate brokers do not write contracts so you will have to hire a special lawyer to do so. Some good news: If you have excellent credit and are well qualified to purchase a home, some banks may actually give you a lenders credit toward your closing costs! Important note: make sure your work history looks good before applying for a mortgage. Most Banks will want to see two years at the same job or consistent employment in the same field, and some banks will not be able to give you a loan if it looks like you have too many gaps in your work history. Some ways around this: Credit Unions like the Actors Credit Union in NYC may be better equipped to understand and take into account your work history as an Artist. Investigate how different banks will respond to your unique work situation as an Artist, and make sure they know everything before you start so that there aren't any surprises during your home buying process.

As I've said before, it's always important to do your research before making any kind of investment and that goes double when talking about Real Estate. The first step is finding a good real estate agent. If you are putting a good chunk of your hard earned money into buying property you want to make sure you are working with someone who has your best interest at heart and will go the extra mile to make sure you are taken care of. Do some digging and if you can, talk to any agents previous clients to see what their experience has been. Once you've found your broker, you must begin to investigate where you want to buy. Find neighborhoods that will be the most desirable for renters. I always look at Downtown areas of cities. College towns can be excellent places to buy rental properties as well. With a little research you can see what areas of most states are prime to buy investment properties. Finally, look at different types of mortgages and zero in on which loan works best for you.

A few other home/apartment buying basics:

Home Inspections

Have your property inspected by a licensed home inspector. Make sure you don't skimp on this part of the home buying process. The inspector may find something that keeps you from buying a money pit or minor things that the seller will agree to fix before you close, but having knowledge about the home you are buying is incredibly important. Even if the property you want to buy is being sold "as is" you should still know what you are getting into.

Earnest Money

Earnest money is a small amount of money you give the seller when you sign the contract to indicate that you are serious about buying their home. It also serves as an incentive for you to stay within the set contractual deadlines for various things like the home inspection, appraisal, and loan objection deadlines. Earnest money is also part of the total down payment for the home.

Homeowners Insurance

It is always imperative that you carry homeowners insurance on any property you buy, and a bank will require that you get a policy in order to secure a mortgage loan. I'll also add that it's not a bad idea to have renters insurance if you live in NYC.

Closing Costs

These are extra costs you will incur when buying a home. Things like loan origination fees, appraisal costs, underwriter fees, administration fees. In NYC closing costs can get very high because of lawyer costs, mansion tax if the property is 1 million or more, and mortgage tax. Make sure you have enough money saved to cover the closing costs in addition to your down payment.

What I've touched on in this section is just the very tip of the iceberg. If Real Estate is something that interests you, make sure you find a good loan officer and real estate broker that can help walk you through everything in detail.

What To Do When it's Time To Sell?

Selling a property can bring you huge profits, but there are also a few things to know before you liquidate your investment. Broker Commissions: When you decided to put a property on the market, remember that the seller almost always pays all broker commissions. This can sometimes be negotiated, but most of the time this expense falls on the seller. How much are we talking about? Well, most real estate brokers charge around 2.8% of the sale price for their services. Multiply that 2.8% by two (for your agent and the buyers) and you are going to look at giving up 5.6% of the purchase price of your property. An Example: Say the property you are selling is listed for $300k, and you get a full price offer and go under contract. 5.6% of $300k is $16,800. That's a big chunk of your profit! You must make sure that you take into account the commissions you will have to pay into the price you are going to list the property for! Especially if you still owe the bank for your mortgage. When you sell the property, any outstanding balance on your loan becomes immediately due. Your bottom dollar sales price, at the very least, needs to cover your initial investment (down payment), the repayment of your mortgage loan, and both brokers commissions. Obviously the goal is to sell the property for much more than the bare minimum, but if that's not possible, try to break even. Though, if you have been renting the property, your tenants have been paying down the mortgage for as long as it's been rented. And while it can take a while to actually make a dent in the principal of the loan, over time you will owe the bank less and less, increasing your chance on making a bigger profit when you sell.

Another factor to consider when selling a property is Capital Gains Tax. If you own the property for less than a year, the IRS will tax whatever profit you make at the same rate they tax your personal income that year. But if you hold it for any amount of time past a year, the max capital gains tax rate is 15%. To use our previous example: Say you bought a property for $250k. You then decide to sell your property after owning it for at least a year for $300k. The IRS will allow you to deduct some of your expenses and commissions before calculating the capital gains tax you have to pay. So to factor that, subtract the 5.6% for commissions ($16,800) which leaves you with $283,200. As far as the IRS is concerned you are making a $33,200 profit on the sale (sales price after expenses - the original purchase price) and if it's before a year you will pay at your same tax rate or if after a year, at a rate of 15%. 15% of $33,200 comes out to $4980, which would leave you with a final profit of $28,220 from the sale. Are there ways to avoid paying this extra tax? Yes there are! When I sold my one bed/ one bath loft in Downtown Denver I did what is called a 1031 Exchange. In layman's terms a 1031 Exchange basically means you are taking the full amount from the sale of one property and "Exchanging" it into another property or properties. There are a few rules surrounding doing a 1031 exchange and there are companies you can hire to help you complete one legally and properly. Make sure you look into doing a 1031 exchange to avoid paying extra taxes on the sale of your property!

In conclusion, real estate can be an excellent investment and bring you a great return on your money, but just make sure you know what you are getting into before you make any decisions.

Chapter Eight

The Stock Market

Did you see "The Wolf of Wall Street"? There's that scene where Leo and Matthew McConnaghy are having lunch and basically McConnaghy explains that the reason for a stocks value is "fugazy" aka no reason at all. As someone who likes to have a hand in whatever I'm investing in, the stock market sort of scares me. I don't like the fact that a company's stock price can fluctuate for no real reason. My personal fears aside, the stock market has been a proven winner over long periods of time, but when it's lost it's lost big. The crash of '29, and the great recession of the 2000's show us how bad it can get when the stock market is down. Investing is essentially a form of gambling and the stock market is no exception. I do invest in the stock market, but as I mentioned before, in something called a Mutual Fund.

Mutual Funds

A Mutual Fund is a grouping of stocks from several different industries. This spreads the risk out so that you are less likely to lose money. For example, say a Mutual Fund has ten different stocks in it: 2 from technology companies, 2 from Agriculture companies, 2 from Manufacturing, 2 from the food service industry, and 2 from the entertainment industry. Now say that 6 out of the ten stocks do really well and their stock goes up, but 4 of the companies stock lose a little value or stay the same. You will still break even or come out ahead. And if one industry really takes a beating, you have 4 others to bail you out.

A good return on investment for a mutual fund is around 5% annually. The one I invest in also pays quarterly dividends (extra money given to the shareholders if the company or mutual fund is doing well) that I can either have paid out or use to buy more shares of the mutual fund. reinvesting the dividends back into the mutual fund is a great way to make sure you don't lose any of your initial investment. How? Well if you buy a few more shares of stock in your mutual fund with the money the fund is generating you aren't putting in any more of your actual money. An Example: I bought 100 shares of a mutual fund at $100 a share, so my initial investment was $10,000. Say the fund pays me a quarterly dividend of $300. If I take that dividend and buy 3 more shares at $100 a share I now have 103 shares. So even if the stock's share price goes down to $98 a share I would still be up about $94 (103 shares at $98 = $10,094.00)

Other Ways to Invest In the Stock Market

Mutual Funds are not the only way to invest in the stock market. My older brother has actually done really well for himself by picking individual stocks and buying them. He does, however, do a LOT of research on the companies before he buys their stock. Again you must do your homework before investing in anything! It really comes down to how much risk you are comfortable with. My older brother tends to be ok with a little more risk than I am, and his investments reflect that, but remember: with zero risk come zero reward. If you don't want to be in charge of picking your stocks you can use a financial advisor from one of the many companies who offer investment services. Places like Edward Jones and Charles Schwab specialize in helping investors find good stocks and mutual funds. Again, before you hand over any of your hard earned money, do your homework. The guy I use worked for some of my family members and I saw first hand that he had put their money in some great funds. Make sure you know what you are getting yourself into, and if something sounds too good to be true; it probably is!

As I said before, the stock market has been a proven good bet, but usually over the long term. And while the money you invest in the stock market is fairly liquid (easy to get out), you will want to consider leaving it in the market long enough to make you money. Yes, some stocks can skyrocket overnight, but for the most part, you will be looking at a lot of ups and downs. You may have heard the saying, "Buy low, Sell high"? That "high" part may take months or even years, so consider leaving your money in for a while before you make that investment.

Chapter Nine

Investing In Small Businesses

Another way to invest your money is by starting or buying into small businesses. One of my favorite TV shows is "The Profit". "The Profit" follows multi millionaire Marcus Lemonis as he buys into failing small businesses and then does his best to make them profitable. While Mr. Lemonis makes investing in small business look easy, in actuality, it takes some serious business savvy and a large amount of cash in the bank to successfully invest in small business. AKA investing in small business is not for the faint of heart! I would encourage you to be wary of anyone, friends, family, etc, who has a business for you to invest in. Doing your due diligence on small business investments is incredibly important as well as being ready to devote a large amount of time to make sure your money is being used properly. Also beware of starting a restaurant or buying into one. Recent studies suggest that 60% of most restaurants fail within the first year, and some studies put that number closer to 90%. In my opinion you would be better off putting your money into a CD or Money Market savings account, than putting any of your cash into a restaurant. There are always exceptions to the rule, but if 6 (or more) out of 10 eateries go under it would seem to be too risky a venture. If someone approaches you about investing in their business, make sure they have a comprehensive business plan that show a specific strategy for how they are going to make money.

Starting your own business

Starting your own small business can be an excellent way to make money. My older brother has done incredibly well for himself in a short amount of time as the owner of his own business. However, if you want to start your own business, make sure you take the time to do adequate market research to find out things like who your customers might be? Is there a need for whatever you want to be selling? How much money is it actually going to cost you to get up and running. You know, with the internet there are a lot of ways to start a successful small business at little or no cost. Online stores like Etsy and Ebay give you the opportunity to sell goods to a world wide market.

I always think it's a good idea to test the waters before devoting a lot of time and effort towards any one thing. I'll explain: I use this method with a lot of my investments, but in this case, if you are thinking about opening an online shop, maybe make one or two of what you plan to sell, put them online and see how they do. If it looks like there is a demand for what you want to produce, great! You've found your customer and price point. But if it seems you have priced your goods too high or there isn't quite as much demand as you hoped, lower your price or go back to the drawing board and start over. Remember, the goal of starting any business is to make money

THE NOT SO STARVING ARTIST

and if you are selling goods and services your goal is to get the highest profit margin you can. (Profit Margin: the amount of money between what the consumer pays and what it costs you to make) For Example: If you are making a dress and it costs you $10 for the material and 4 hours of labor at say $20 an hour (if it's you doing the sewing the labor cost can be flexible, but if you get to the point where someone else is doing it you have to factor in the actual labor cost) your total cost per dress is $90. If you sell the dress for $180 your profit margin is 50%. If you could get your material and or labor costs down your profit margin goes up. The more time you can spend plotting out what your costs will be vs. what you could make the better off and less surprised you'll be! I would also say this: always think of the low end of what you expect to sell your goods for. If you can live with the low end and still have a good profit margin, you are setting yourself up for success. That way, if your goods sell for more you will really be making great money!

THE NOT SO STARVING ARTIST

I know I'm a broken record at this point, but do your homework, and maybe doubly so on small business investing/starting, before pulling the trigger on any investment. Know the risks, know the potential return, and make an informed decision.

I hope I've been able to introduce you to some good ways to invest your money and that by reading this book, you will start to take a deeper look at how to put your money to work for you. As I've said many times throughout this book, ALWAYS do your homework on any type of investment before you commit any money. And please, please, please, don't just take my word for any of this. Use the tools around you (internet, friends, colleagues, financial advisors) to learn more and dig deeper into the wide wide world of investing. And again, remember that you aren't going to be financially independent overnight, but (cheesy) every journey of a thousand miles begins with a single step (so cheesy). It's true though, and finishing this book was that first step. Hell, even taking the time to think about any of this was the first step. Now keep going!

Chapter Ten

Money Maps

As I said earlier, I wanted to provide you with a few more Money Maps as well as a Notes section. I would encourage you to fill out the money maps even if you think you know exactly how much you spend every month. You may be surprised to find some hidden costs you can lower. I would also encourage you to take notes on what I've said and start brainstorming the ways you would like to invest your money. The sooner you start practicing good financial habits and saving and investing your money, the sooner you will be able to start taking steps toward financial independence!

THE NOT SO STARVING ARTIST

MY MONEY MAP

WHAT I BRING HOME AFTER TAXES PER WEEK

WEEK 1:_____

WEEK 2:_____

WEEK 3:_____

WEEK 4:_____

TOTAL EARNINGS: _____

10% FOR SAVINGS:_____

MY FIXED COSTS

RENT:_____

THE NOT SO STARVING ARTIST

AVERAGE UTILITIES:_____

TRANSPORTATION:_____

AVERAGE PHONE/INTERNET:_____

INSURANCE (medical/hazard):_____
DEBT REPAYMENT:_____

VARIABLE COSTS

GROCERIES:_____
EATING OUT:_____

ENTERTAINMENT:_____

MISCELLANEOUS (clothes, business expenses, etc):_____

TOTALS

THE NOT SO STARVING ARTIST

TOTAL INCOME AFTER TAXES/
SAVINGS:_____

—

TOTAL FIXED COSTS:_____

TOTAL VARIABLE COSTS:_____

=

AMOUNT LEFT OVER:_____

_____
_____

MY MONEY MAP

WHAT I BRING HOME AFTER TAXES PER WEEK

THE NOT SO STARVING ARTIST

WEEK 1:_____

WEEK 2:_____

WEEK 3:_____

WEEK 4:_____

TOTAL EARNINGS: _____

10% FOR SAVINGS:_____

MY FIXED COSTS

RENT:_____

AVERAGE UTILITIES:_____

TRANSPORTATION:_____

AVERAGE PHONE/INTERNET:_____

THE NOT SO STARVING ARTIST

INSURANCE (medical/hazard):_____
DEBT REPAYMENT:_____

VARIABLE COSTS

GROCERIES:_____
EATING OUT:_____

ENTERTAINMENT:_____

MISCELLANEOUS (clothes, business expenses, etc):_____

TOTALS

TOTAL INCOME AFTER TAXES/
SAVINGS:_____

—

TOTAL FIXED COSTS:_____

THE NOT SO STARVING ARTIST

TOTAL VARIABLE COSTS:_____

=

AMOUNT LEFT OVER:_____

_____
_____

MY MONEY MAP

WHAT I BRING HOME AFTER TAXES PER WEEK

WEEK 1:_____

WEEK 2:_____

WEEK 3:_____

WEEK 4:_____

THE NOT SO STARVING ARTIST

TOTAL EARNINGS: _____

10% FOR SAVINGS:_____

MY FIXED COSTS

RENT:_____

AVERAGE UTILITIES:_____

TRANSPORTATION:_____

AVERAGE PHONE/INTERNET:_____

INSURANCE (medical/hazard):_____
DEBT REPAYMENT:_____

VARIABLE COSTS

GROCERIES:_____
EATING OUT:_____

THE NOT SO STARVING ARTIST

ENTERTAINMENT:_____

MISCELLANEOUS (clothes, business expenses, etc):_____

TOTALS

TOTAL INCOME AFTER TAXES/
SAVINGS:_____

—

TOTAL FIXED COSTS:_____

TOTAL VARIABLE COSTS:_____

=

AMOUNT LEFT OVER:_____

THE NOT SO STARVING ARTIST

MY MONEY MAP

WHAT I BRING HOME AFTER TAXES PER WEEK

WEEK 1:_____

WEEK 2:_____

WEEK 3:_____

WEEK 4:_____

TOTAL EARNINGS: _____

10% FOR SAVINGS:_____

MY FIXED COSTS

RENT:_____

AVERAGE UTILITIES:_____

THE NOT SO STARVING ARTIST

TRANSPORTATION:_____

AVERAGE PHONE/INTERNET:_____

INSURANCE (medical/hazard):_____
DEBT REPAYMENT:_____

VARIABLE COSTS

GROCERIES:_____
EATING OUT:_____

ENTERTAINMENT:_____

MISCELLANEOUS (clothes, business expenses, etc):_____

TOTALS

TOTAL INCOME AFTER TAXES/
SAVINGS:_____

THE NOT SO STARVING ARTIST

—

TOTAL FIXED COSTS:_____

TOTAL VARIABLE COSTS:_____

=

AMOUNT LEFT OVER:_____

Notes

_____

_____

_____

_____

THE NOT SO STARVING ARTIST

THE NOT SO STARVING ARTIST

THE NOT SO STARVING ARTIST

THE NOT SO STARVING ARTIST

_____

_____

_____

_____

_____

_____

_____

_____

_____

_____

THE NOT SO STARVING ARTIST

_____

_____

_____

_____

_____

_____

_____

_____

_____

_____

THE NOT SO STARVING ARTIST

_____

_____

_____

_____

_____

_____

_____

_____

_____

_____

_____

THE NOT SO STARVING ARTIST

_____

_____

_____

_____

_____

_____

_____

_____

_____

_____

THE NOT SO STARVING ARTIST

_____

_____

_____

_____

_____

_____

_____

_____

_____

_____

THE NOT SO STARVING ARTIST

_____

_____

_____

_____

_____

_____

_____

_____

_____

_____

THE NOT SO STARVING ARTIST

_____

_____

_____

_____

_____

_____

_____

_____

_____

_____

_____

_____

Made in the USA
Middletown, DE
06 October 2016